I0465501

Seena Zarie is currently working in Dubai Electricity and Water Authority. He is mainly focusing on the following two subjects: positivity and self-development. He wrote many online books on several subjects and has a personal blog in Arabic called (*Be Positive* and *Make Life*) which represents his personal motto in life. This blog contains different articles focusing mainly on positivity and self-development.

I would like to dedicate this book to all those who supported me in writing this book.

Seena Zarie

100 X 100

100 Ways Towards Happiness at Work

AUSTIN MACAULEY PUBLISHERS™

LONDON · CAMBRIDGE · NEW YORK · SHARJAH

ISBN – 9789948348054 – (Paperback)
ISBN – 9789948348412 – (E-Book)

Application Number: MC-10-01-5798828
Age Classification: E

First Published (2020)
AUSTIN MACAULEY PUBLISHERS FZE
Sharjah Publishing City
P.O Box [519201]
Sharjah, UAE
www.austinmacauley.ae
+971 655 95 202

Thanks to my organization, Dubai Electricity and Water Authority (DEWA) who provided and ensured happiness for all its employees.

Thanks to all my leaders, managers and colleagues from whom I learnt many ways of happiness.

Special thanks to my wife who reviewed this book and provided valuable comments and feedback.

Thanks to all people I learnt happiness from, either directly or indirectly.

Table of Contents

Introduction

Happiness is a **main goal** for everyone in life. Work places are also focusing on happiness among their employees. Recently, many countries started to organize conferences and summits about happiness in the work place. This means that happiness became an **essential concept** and requirement rather than being an optional one.

Throughout my work experience, I learnt many ways for applying happiness in work either by seeing different tools in my organization or by reading or hearing other people's experiences through conferences, news, articles, friends...etc.

I tried to gather these tools in one book to be a reference for any organization that aims to spread happiness among its employees.

What Is New in This Book?

I know that many wrote about this subject before, and so thought about writing it somehow in a different way from existing ones so that the reader will reach to the point in a simpler way.

I chose to name the book (**100X100**) where the first 100 is **100 different ways** to achieve happiness at the work place and the second 100 means **around 100 words** in each paragraph.

My objective is mainly to open the reader's mind about the mentioned tools without going into a lot of depth, which in turn then gives the opportunity to readers to search more about each tool.

What Is Happiness in Workplace?

It is not easy to define happiness in the workplace as there are **different definitions** or ways of **what makes employees happy at workplace**. Some employees will be happy by promotions while others will be happy while winning awards. Another group will be happy when they are empowered.

Because of that, there should be different tools to make employees happy. This can be measured through different mediums such as surveys or feedbacks. Having results is the best evidence; opinions are not much of value.

Happiness should be a priority for each organization since it will lead to great results.

Is There 100% Happiness at Workplace?

In my opinion, the answer is **no**. If we reach to a point where we achieved 100% happiness, we will stop thinking of new ways and methods. This might affect the happiness level at work causing it to be reduced since employees like to always see new updates and surprises.

I believe that there are always more ways than what I will mention in this book as happiness is supposed to be a continuous subject, and hence it means that there will always be new initiatives and ways. Still, this book shall cover many different ways of finding happiness at the workplace.

(Important Notice)

It is important to know, before mentioning the ways for 'achieving happiness at work', that these are **not prioritized**. The decision of importance for any specific 'way' depends on the organization and the leadership.

The responsibility of implementing happiness in any way is **distributed amongst everyone;** some of them are expected to be done by the leaders and managers, while others are to be done by employees themselves and sometimes by teamwork. This cooperation in implementation of happiness will lead to happiness of everyone eventually.

It is important to have **dedicated** departments or committees for happiness. Nevertheless, each employee in the organization despite his or her level, has a big role in the organization's happiness.

1: Happiness Culture

Building happiness culture among employees means that the organization is really caring about happiness. I believe that we should make happiness the **DNA** of the organization. This needs strong efforts from all concerns especially from organization's leadership.

There are a variety of ways mentioned in this book that will support building this strong culture. One of the important questions that supports building this strong culture is: **Why do we need happiness?** If everyone in the organization is able to answer this question, we can say that we are on the right track of achieving happiness among all employees in the organization.

2: Happiness Value

One of the main considerations to build happiness culture in the organization is by **feeling the importance of happiness** by all employees especially higher management. The higher management has an important role in ensuring happiness through relating it to every activity and event. Also, they should continuously deliver happiness messages to all employees through different internal and external channels.

It is important also to conduct **happiness surveys** and announce the results among employees, followed by setting actions to recover any gap.

By establishing a **dedicated** team or department for employees' happiness alongside launching team **happiness awards** can support the value of happiness in the organization.

3: Happiness Strategy

Strategy is the direction for achieving visions. Happiness also requires a **clear strategy** in order to be achieved. This strategy will mainly define how happiness will be implemented and realized.

The importance of strategy comes from ensuring that happiness will be **an integral part** of the organization and not only remembered in certain occasions or special events. Also, it will allow continuous improvement and evaluation since strategies are reviewed periodically.

Happiness can be part of an organization's vision, mission or values which will support the **real implementation** of happiness in the organization since it will be always on leadership agenda.

4: Happiness Framework

Maslow's Pyramid for human needs is a good example for a framework. It can also be used as organization's happiness framework.

Happiness framework will define **the areas of happiness** which an organization needs to concentrate on with reference to the happiness strategy. For example, the organization will achieve happiness through four main aspects: Programs, culture, knowledge and employee benefits.

The importance of this framework is that it will **direct the thinking** of all concerns towards achieving happiness in specific areas. Also, it will open the mind for many initiatives, programs and innovation towards achieving happiness among concerns.

5: Happiness Programs

Having a clear strategy and framework are important, but employees finally need to see the **outcomes**. An attempt to achieve happiness through different programs show direct efforts of management and that is what employees want to see.

Custodian of conducting these programs must take into consideration that there are **different needs** so there should be different programs according to these needs. Studying employees' needs or what will make them happy shall greatly help in planning these programs.

Programs are always recommended to be **innovative** since employees want to see them. If any program is successful, there will be no harm to repeat it.

6: Happiness Index

Any organization can say that its employees are happy, but how can it prove that and what is the level of this happiness? Based on the famous rule (**What can't be measured, can't be managed**), happiness also should have clear measures in order to know the organization's status and level of real happiness.

Happiness index is a very useful tool to **prove** happiness within the organization. There is currently an international happiness index for countries. Organizations can introduce a similar index. It is important to have **targets** for the organization to achieve. Also, announcing the index yearly for all employees will be useful.

7: Happiness Dashboard

Monitoring happiness level in the organization is important. This can be achieved in a new smart way through Dashboard. Dashboards are a series of illustrative charts and diagrams design to report highlights and key results of the work to leaders or top management.

As happiness is one of the keys to organizational success, it should also be an integral part of the management dashboard. It can be also shown to all employees to know their real happiness level.

Dashboards should represent the **realistic status** of happiness in the organization. These figures and statistics are important for decision making, improvements, benchmarking, and getting awards.

8: Happiness Pulse

One of the useful tools applied in some organizations is the happiness pulse. This pulse will show **happiness level** of the employee in a certain day. This pulse can be sent through email or can be available in smart devices in different locations so that employees can select their happiness status (happy, unhappy or neutral).

This pulse will **remind** employees about happiness. More importantly, it helps taking **action** after the pulse is sent. For example, one of the organizations instructed its managers to meet with their employees who sent unhappy pulses. This will support increasing happiness or at least send a message regarding the importance of happiness.

9: Happiness Studies and Statistics

One of the main tools which will support happiness is having **continuous internal and external** studies and statistics about happiness. It will be useful to share some of them among employees, but more importantly, it will bring to the attention of leadership and top management regarding latest happiness news and relevant insights.

These studies and statistics will support conducting new programs and taking better decisions. Scientific studies are important to **open minds** about new techniques for achieving employees' happiness.

The organization can make **agreements** with universities or study centers to provide latest study results or even conduct customized happiness studies on the organization itself.

10: Happiness Surveys

Surveys are supportive tools to measure **actual conditions**. Many leaders take decisions based on survey results. However, it is not very much recommended to do so since survey results are not that much accurate. They can be a supportive tool but not the base for assessing happiness.

Happiness surveys should be **designed carefully** to provide accurate results as much as possible. Also, there should be mechanisms to identify real answers from employees since some of them answer randomly in order to just get the survey done.

Leaders should remind employees about the **importance** of filling surveys accurately since the results will affect all.

11: Vision / Mission

Having a vision and mission has become a normal practice for any organization. The challenging part is **the effectiveness** of these visions and missions; how they are communicated to the employees and whether employees are really working to achieve them or not?

Knowing where to go will make someone happy and the opposite is also true. When the employee does not know why he or she is performing a certain task or why the organization is planning and executing certain projects or initiatives, it will cause unhappiness to the employees.

It is always important to **relate** all works, projects and initiatives to the vision and mission.

12: Smiling

There is strong relation between happiness and smiling. **The happiness icon** is always represented with a smile.

Smiling is not a policy or regulation or something forced on employees; although I heard some organizations do that with customer front line employees. Instead, smiling should be a **culture** in the organization where we should see everyone smiling. This smile comes as a reflection of internal and external happiness.

Organizations should always **promote** smiling. Leaders and managers should be **examples** for smiling. Also, there should be a mechanism in reminding the staff to constantly put on a smile.

13: Leadership

The role of organization's leadership in achieving happiness is very important or let us say is the most important. Leaders are responsible for **establishing happiness strategy and framework** and continuously following up in order to improve and evaluate happiness among employees.

More importantly, a leader should be an **example** for employees. Leaders should spread happiness around them, participate with employees in different programs, conduct some happiness programs and provide initiatives for increasing happiness.

Leadership **support** for any program and initiative is very important. If you want to feel the importance of this support, imagine the opposite; less support or even none. Will there be happiness?

14: Managers

The role of managers in achieving happiness is not less than leaders since they are more in touch with employees and they are the ones who apply strategic directions and objectives.

The managers should be **good facilitators** for any happiness programs. Their **good example** will support greatly in achieving happiness. Also, managers have a great role in organizing happiness events and activities for their employees.

Managers are the **main communication** between employees and leadership; therefore, if any disturbance occurs in this channel, the happiness level will be affected. Leaders should always care about managers' happiness since their happiness will reflect on employees'.

15: Values

Values are **reflections** of what is important in the organization. Organizations can have different values according to their area of responsibility. However, it is important for employees to feel that these values are **really applied** within organization.

If the organization has an (innovation) value for example, the employees should see that the organization is caring and focusing on innovation and innovators. The moment that the employee will feel that a value is not really implemented or being practiced, complains will be raised.

Selection of the values should be done after studies and studying feedbacks from stakeholders.

16: Reputation

Each organization cares about its reputation. Employees will be always happier if their organization's reputation is high. This reputation is **built** through several years. Think about all the famous and successful organizations. How much they took to build this reputation?

Building a high reputation comes from several factors. Winning local or international awards is an important factor. Having talent and distinguished employees is another one. Achieving high results and profits is also important and so on.

Employees will be **proud** to work for these kinds of organizations. At the same time, organizations will attract other good employees who can add more value to the organization.

17: Motivation

Motivation is needed for everyone in the organization starting from top leaders up to lower grade employees. There are many **motivation tools** and it is important to vary them since what motivates one employee differs from what motivates the other.

Motivation is always expected **from top to bottom** and should not be linked to specific time. It should part of leaders' and managers' culture.

If you want to feel the motivation of employees notice their faces when they come to work. Many insights can be realized at that time. Motivated employees will always be happy to go to work.

18: Self-Motivation

Beside external motivation from others, it is essential to have self-motivation in order to **sustain the happiness**. Self-motivation is the **force** that drives you to do things without any external effect.

There are many ways to **gain** self-motivation such as setting and writing objectives and making achievements that are self-rewarding.

It is important for employees to **learn** how to be self-motivated since there are many factors which may affect an employee's happiness such as less appreciation, no promotions and negative feedbacks. All of these are expected in a work environment; so, having self-motivation will reduce the negative effects of them.

19: Appreciation

Appreciation is a powerful motivational tool. It simply means **"Thank you"** to any effort done. This "Thank you" can be gifts, certificates, or emails from any leader or manger sending a message that an employee's efforts are realized and appreciated. Of course, the value of the appreciation will be higher as the giving person is higher in position.

Organizations with higher appreciation level towards their employees will have higher happiness rate. This practice should be part of leaders and managers culture.

Addition of surprise element to employees' appreciation in front of colleagues will also double its value in multiple folds.

20: Awards

Awards are effective tools used for thanking distinguished employees. Organizations should provide **more chances** for their distinguished employees to get awards. This can be achieved through having different awards categories for individuals, groups and special achievements.

Departments within organizations can have internal awards. This will provide more chances for employees to exhibit their achievements and prepare themselves for bigger awards.

It is valuable to nominate employees for **local or international awards** outside the organization as it will motivate employees. Also, it is important to note that organization **top leaders** should always be available during awards ceremony to personally hand over the awards directly to employees.

21: Surprises

A nice surprise is always a source of happiness for most employees if not all of them. Imagine that an employee reaches office and finds a letter of thanks from his manager or an employee joins work after a long break and finds a ceremony welcoming him.

We can provide many examples for these kinds of nice surprises. Surely, employees will be happy; not only those who are targeted by the surprise but also those who organized it or provided support.

These surprises will heavily depend on the **level of relationship** among employees. If the relationship is strong, more nice surprises will occur.

22: Trust

Trust is one of the important values that any employee requires. It is something **bi-directional** between leaders and employees.

Organizations which have high **trust level** will be happier. Why? Firstly, respect will exist among all in terms of personalities and opinions. Secondly, everyone will support each other and that will lead to better decisions, motivation and production.

Everyone likes to be trusted. It is a source for **positive energy**. One of trust's ways is assigning **responsibilities** no matter how big or difficult they are since there will be a support always. Another way is announcing success among all and avoiding blame in case of failures.

23: Empowerment

Empowerment means giving full responsibilities to someone else. It is a **motivational tool** and a healthy practice in developed organizations. Empowerment will send a message to leaders to **trust** in others. Also, it is a tool for **preparing new leaders** in the organization.

Empowerment should have a clear mechanism so that the proposed empowered employees should get **enough trainings and knowledge** before getting full empowerment in order not to affect the work.

Empowerment is **not a gift** given to anyone. It is something given to hard workers and distinguished employees. It is a way to thank their efforts and motivate them for better performance.

24: Job Rotation

Job rotation is a process where employees will be shifted to another job for a certain period. It has many purposes. One of them is to train leaders and managers for **new responsibilities** which can be part of improving and empowering them.

It can be also done for employees as part of training them or sometimes as a **change**. This rotation has many benefits especially if it is with new teams. Besides learning new things, it can also build **relationship** depending on employees' personalities.

New graduated employees can have opportunities also for rotation among different sections.

25: Team Work

Working in teams is common in any organization since many objectives cannot be achieved individually. It is important to have the **culture of successful teamwork** amongst employees. Working in a bad teamwork environment will lead to decreased happiness.

There are many **elements for successful teamwork** such as effective leadership, good communication, clear responsibilities and cooperation among members.

There are many other elements as well; however, the most important aspect is knowing the **objective** of this team. Knowing the objective will make each member effective in the team. This effectiveness is a source for successful teamwork and happiness.

26: Work Environment

When an employee is asked about his happiness in the work place, one of his criteria or a reference in deciding this happiness will be his work environment.

The work environment includes many things such as **relations with managers** – of which I believe is the most important alongside relations with colleagues, policies and regulations, office arrangements, facilities…etc. Many of the topics that I will mention in this book fall under work environment.

One of areas that make **Google** as reference for others is its great work environment. Leadership should give **priority** for the work environment's happiness level and improve it in continuous matter though different policies and initiatives.

27: Healthy Competition

Competition is something common within any organization. Having **internal awards** will usually increase the competition among employees and departments. There will be also competition in achieving results, minimizing complains, surveys results...etc.

This competition is a **healthy practice** since it will raise the organization level in many fields. The important point is to have a **healthy competition environment**. Leaders and managers should always be an **example** for others. This healthy competition will not affect any relationship or cooperation among employees.

All employees should remember that they are **one family** working for the same organization and any problem due to unfriendly competition will affect the organization.

28: Ethics

One of the important factors for a happy environment is the **existence of good ethics** among employees. This point is very clear and anyone can compare between a work environment with ethics and another one without it.

Organizations have an important role to remind employees about work ethics, but the main role is played by **employees themselves**. This will depend much on education at home and school. Still, the employee can force himself to apply ethics at work.

Leaders and managers should be an **example** in applying ethics for all employees. There should also be **policies** in the organization for dealing with bad ethics within work.

29: Relationship

Relationship among employees' is an important source for happiness. Imagine that an employee is going to work and has a problem with a manager or a colleague. Will he be happy that day? **Good relationships mean happiness**.

Organizations should always ensure that relationships among employees are healthy. Leaders and managers have the main role to do that and they should be good **examples** for all and avoid any relationship disturbance. Good relationships must exist among all levels.

Employees should know that **relationship problems** can occur at any time, but they shouldn't allow these problems to become big and disturb their happiness.

30: Enjoyment

Feeling the joy during work is a strong sign of happiness. This enjoyment comes from **many factors**. Friendly environment at work, good relations with managers and leaders, and social activities are some factors for this enjoyment.

If the employee feels enjoyed, he will be **more productive and happier** during work. How many employees wake up in the morning and enjoy the fact that they will go to work? I think the number is not significant.

The organization has an important role to spread this feeling of enjoyment. Leaders and managers have an important role also, but I believe the main source of it comes from the **employees' themselves**.

31: Differences

I mean here **differences in opinion**. What is the problem and how is it related with happiness? The problem is that some employees don't realize that differences in opinions are **something normal and even healthy**. They think that others should listen and follow whatever they say or suggest.

When employees don't realize that, it will affect their happiness level since they will think that others are against them or nobody is listening to them.

This is an issue related to **culture** and that is where differences are normally expected. However, organizations can spread awareness among employees about this phenomenon in order not to affect their happiness.

32: Disappointment

Disappointment is something **negative** which can happen to any employee for any reason. More disappointments to the employee means lower happiness.

Employees should know **how to deal** with disappointments or at least be trained for that. If leaders and manager can do something, they should do it immediately. The objective is always to move the employee from this negative feeling.

If there is a group disappointment, there should be **immediate meetings** followed by actions from leaders or managers. Employees should see that their leaders and managers **care** about them. This will reduce the disappointment level.

33: Worry

Being worried is another **negative** point in a work environment especially if leaders or managers are sources of this worry. Some employees get worried if they meet their managers or receive calls and emails from them always expecting that something negative shall be received from them. This means that **trust** does not exist between managers and employees.

Leaders and managers shouldn't spread these kinds of worries. Instead, they can be close to employees, announce positive things, encourage and support employees and smile all the time. This will reduce or remove **barriers** between them and employees that shall reduce worry and increase trust and happiness.

34: Pressure

I mean here the **negative pressure** which affects employee's performance and happiness. This pressure will come sometimes from managers who will assign **additional responsibilities** and tasks to employees. However, it can also come from employees themselves by not organizing their tasks. This pressure can cause a bad effect on employees.

It is the manager's responsibility not to put pressure on employees. **Employees themselves** should also inform managers if they are under pressure. Of course, there should be acceptable reasons for this pressure and not only from normal duties or a little bit more. Employees should learn how to deal with pressures and overcome them.

35: Office

An employee's office is considered as his **second home**. If we count the hours that an employee stays in his office, we will realize this fact. Seven or eight hours per day is not a short time. There are some employees who are working most of their time out of office yet some of them have offices also.

The office should **spread happiness** also. Some organizations have started to focus on its employee's office, the design, colors, facilities…etc. since it can be a source of happiness. Again, it is like a home so the employee should **feel happy** when he/she comes to the office.

36: Innovation

Under this point, it is important to focus on building **innovation culture** among employees. This can be achieved through different tools such as awareness, supporting organization's innovators and innovations and having an effective suggestion system.

It is important also to participate in **international innovation awards**. This will provide feelings that the organization is supporting innovation. This is besides **internal innovation awards**. Also, organizing and participating in innovation conferences and exhibitions is equally as important.

Innovation is a **world trend**, and so when employees feel that their organizations support innovation, they shall be happy and proud that the organization is on track with world trends.

37: Suggestion Systems

One of points that I have noticed which affects happiness is the **existence and effectiveness** of an organization's suggestion system. Why? Because employees want a **systematic channel** to share their suggestions. Also, the existence of a suggestion system is evidence that the organization **supports** innovators and innovations.

Besides having easy steps to submit a suggestion there should be a **clear process** for submitting suggestions, evaluating them, and replying to the submitter with the result. The process should define number of days required for each step. When any of these steps are not followed or there is deviation in the process, it will affect employees' happiness.

38: Brainstorming Sessions

Brainstorming sessions is another channel for **providing suggestions**. It is important to have **effective sessions** by having clear objectives. An official brainstorming session has a methodology, but the main criteria is having output from this session.

Giving **equal opportunities** to all for suggesting will make the session effective. In fact, the effectiveness part comes from the **variety** of employees' backgrounds, working fields, experiences, and nationalities.

I have personally run many brainstorming sessions and I noticed the level of employees' interactions. Not all employees' like to participate and provide suggestions, yet there are some who like these sessions and feel happy with them.

39: Communication

Communication is needed amongst all levels in the organization. It is important to have **different channels** for communicating messages such as emails, memos, awareness, speeches...etc. Having different channels is always better since an employee's understanding and preference of any message is different.

More important is the **effectiveness** of communication among employees. This will include providing an organization's latest news, accurate information and passing important information to all.

Having an effective communication among **leaders and employees** is an essential element for happiness. When employees know that leaders listen to them and when leaders know that they will get effective feedback, everyone will be happy.

40: Organization Objectives

Having objectives is important for personal success in life. The same concept applies to organizations. Objectives will provide employees a **clear picture** of organization's direction.

How this will affect an employee's happiness level? Imagine that an employee doesn't know where the organization is going? Is it achieving its objectives or not? Saying **no** to any of these questions means something is wrong and the issue will get worse if external parties know more than employees about an organization's objectives.

Communicating the above information to employees is important. Also, **inviting** employees for setting or evaluating objectives will be an additional source of happiness.

41: Employee's Objectives

Besides an organization's objective, individual objectives are important also. Employees feel happy if they know what is expected from them. This will also **challenge** them to achieve more than what is expected from them which will be another source for happiness.

An employee's objectives should be **related** to an organization's objectives. This will make employees feel that they are part of the big family.

The concept of **SMART(ER)*** objectives is famous worldwide and it will help employees to know exactly what to do. Still, there should be always an area for **innovation** and social activities that will finally benefit the organization and the employee.

* SMARTER: S = Specific, M = Measurable, A = Achievable, R = Realistic, T = Time Bounded, E = Evaluated, R = Rewarded.

42: Responsibility

It is well known that each employee in the organization has specific responsibilities. Employees should feel the **importance** of these responsibilities since each responsibility – even if considered small, will achieve something for the organization.

If each employee performs his responsibilities well, it shall be **reflected** at the organization level. The opposite is also true. Many of an organization's failure comes from a lack of responsibilities.

Responsibilities should be **clear** for the employee from day one and this will be usually mentioned in the job description. **Additional responsibilities** will be there always. They should be also clear and informed well to employees.

43: Job Description

Job description is necessary for any employee to define **clear responsibilities** and to know what is his role in the organization. Knowing what to do will make employees happier by clearing the grey area.

Some organizations will define different **categories** in the job description such as main tasks and competencies. It is important for the employees to know the job description.

Some employees will stick to their job descriptions only, while others will have a **larger scope** by being assigned additional tasks or volunteering for other tasks. Still, doing what is required from employees in the job description is the key.

44: Social Responsibility

One of the concepts introduced recently by organizations' is social responsibility which means providing **useful things to society** such as helping the poor, patients, disabled or, elderly people in society. This is of course besides what is organization's core business.

Participating in these events will add **value** to the organization and employees know where they can make others happy. This can be considered as one of the biggest sources of happiness.

Big organizations nowadays **announce** their social responsibility's contributions to prove that they are active in the society and they are close to people. This will surely be a source of pride for the employees.

45: Volunteering

Volunteering is not part of an employees' job; still some organizations provide chances for their employees to volunteer in many activities as it will add **value** to both organization, its employees and will increase the happiness level.

The feeling of volunteering is wonderful and this is well known for those who participate in these activities, since they are doing the work from **their own** without any force. This is besides the feelings of helping or providing services to others.

The organization's role is to **encourage** its employees to volunteer in different activities either those organized by the organization or by external parties.

46: Makings Others Happy

One of the greatest sources for happiness is making others happy. This can be done on both individual and organization levels.

I want to focus more on **leaders and managers** since one of their main tasks is to make employees happy. This can be done through different initiatives such as celebrating employees' successes, welcoming employees after leaves, visiting patients, consolations…etc.

Organizations can also contribute in **providing chances** to employees to make others happy either in the work place or society. The feeling of seeing others smiling is very satisfying and it shall generate **positive energy** in the employee which means more productivity.

47: Excellence

Employees will be proud when they **feel and live** excellence in the organization. Being referenced by others as an excellent organization means a lot to employees.

Excellence means being the best or distinguished. This will need **big efforts** from everyone. These efforts may raise complaints from some; however, most employees will feel happy when applying excellence especially if positive results and awards are expected.

Excellence is a **culture** which should be embedded in the organization. This is mainly the rule of leaderships; yet, everyone should cooperate to achieve it. It is also important to motivate and award excellent employees and departments.

48: Challenges

Our assumption is that challenges are sources for worries. In fact, it is the opposite. Employees **like challenges** especially the distinguished ones. The happiness comes when these challenges are overcome and the employees are appreciated.

Being distinguished means **more challenges**, so there should be always **encouragements** to take more challenges and appreciate whoever overcomes them. On the other hand, there should be a place always for **accepting failures**. By this way, challenges will be source of happiness.

Announcing the challenge stories and how they are overcome will motivate the employees as it will show that they are distinguished.

49: Achievements

One of the main sources of happiness is achievement on either an individual or organizational level. Employees should feel that any kind of **positive achievement** is a source of happiness even if it is a small one. This culture is important since some people think that achievement should be always big.

Achievement is a source for **self-motivation** also. It is the rule of leaders and mangers to appreciate employees' achievements. This can be done through different channels such as awards, announcing the achievements, promotions…etc.

The culture of promoting achievements will motivate all to achieve more and will lead to more happiness.

50: Positivity

Simply, I define positivity as **good feelings leading to good work**. Positivity is linked strongly with happiness where good feelings and work will lead to happiness. Positivity should be a part of an organization's **culture**. Leaders are the most important part in building this culture through being good **examples** to all employees whether through their words or actions.

Encouragement for positivity should exist and appreciating or awarding positive staff or work shall be better.

Complaining does not conflict with positivity, however the important point is to take an action, provide a solution or generate an idea to overcome any problem. This is positivity.

51: Optimism

Being optimistic is a part of positivity. It is something which organizations should concentrate on. This will come through different factors. One of the important factors is related directly to **leaders and managers**. They should be an **example** for being optimistic especially during problems and crisis.

Being optimistic is **not only** saying words, but actions, hard work and achieving results. Of course, what is said is important but employees always look into what is done more than what is said.

Optimism should be **built** among employees, and those who try to spread negativity should be stopped and even cornered if it continues.

52: Knowledge Sharing

Imagine that employees are gaining new knowledge on a regular basis. Their happiness will be more than an employee who feels that knowledge is hidden. Sharing knowledge will spread **team work culture** where everyone cares that others should benefit from whatever they have.

Organizations with strong knowledge and sharing of culture will have **stronger** employees than others who don't, as everyone will try to benefit others with something and the result will be that all will gain different knowledge from different fields. This is also an important source for **innovation and improvement**.

Having **awards** for knowledge sharing will motivate employees to share more with innovative ways.

53: Knowledge Centers / Libraries

I consider having knowledge centers or libraries in an organization something valuable since it is a **great opportunity** for getting knowledge and reading books. Employees should be proud and get maximum benefits of such centers and libraries.

Some organizations have also **smart libraries** with e-books. Others will make a **partnership** with famous universities or libraries to access their products and books to give employees opportunities to read or get certain required information.

Besides having these libraries, they should be **effective** ones. This can be through organizing events and activities in these libraries to ensure that maximum number of employees know about them and visit them.

54: Social Activities

Going out of a work environment periodically is necessary for employees since it will reduce **work pressure**, open their mind for new things and strengthen their social relations. These are the main objectives for social activities and is a welcoming change.

Social activities are an **effective way** if leaders want to deliver certain massages related to work in different ways such as playing games, breakfast, lunch, tours, visits…etc. These messages will be remembered always especially if they were something innovative.

It is important for all leaders to **participate** in these activities with employees. This will break many obstacles between them.

55: Meetings

Meetings are essential for any employee. The rate of meetings will be more so long as the employee is in a higher position. We should ensure that meetings are a **source of happiness and** not the opposite.

Unfortunately, I saw many employees who are unhappy because of meetings. This is mainly because of **ineffective meetings** which can be due to many reasons such as not starting or ending on time, many side or unwanted discussions, not following the agenda and no role of the employee in the meeting.

If we are able to convert all above points to be positive, we can get an **effective** meeting.

56: Rules and Policies

Any organization will have rules and policies. Rules and policies should be there to **help and facilitate,** not be an obstacle. Employees will be happy if they see that these rules and policies are benefiting them and organizing things. It is important for these rules and policies to be **transparent**, clear and available when requested.

Fairness while applying these rules and policies should exist. Otherwise, employees will feel unsatisfied. There will be surely some **special cases** where rules and policies won't be applicable; still there should be **control** on these cases. Alternatively, it will cause complaints among employees.

57: Promotions

Promotions is a way to appreciate and motivate distinguished employees which will lead to more happiness among them. **Promotion mechanisms** should be clear and known by all; otherwise, many question marks and complains will be raised by employees.

Fairness while promoting is necessary. Employees who deserve promotions should be promoted. Again, clear promotion mechanism and criteria will help managers to decide promotions. Managers should always have **answers** for promoting or not promoting any employee.

It should also be clear for any promoted employee that this promotion is **not the end**. It should be a source for more energy and happiness.

58: Salary

Getting a good salary is on **top priority** for most employees. Actually, many employees seek for new opportunities to get a better salary. Salary should be **defined well** for employees from the first day. In most of the cases, HR representatives do that during the interview. In addition to that, any **increments** should be defined also if possible.

Employees will care so much if their salaries are being changed for reasons such as being either increased or being cut. The second one is more critical, and so it should be always **justified**. There should be other ways for salary increments since it is important for happiness.

59: Bonus

Bonus is something provided by some organizations to their staff due to high profits, performance, getting special awards or can be a part of organization policy.

Providing a bonus is a great source of happiness for employees especially if it is **unexpected**. It is a powerful thanking message to all employees **appreciating their efforts**.

Bonus can be money or additional leave days or any additional things that have value. An important point which should be considered is the **fairness** during distribution of the bonus amount to employees. The policy of distribution should be clear to all in order to avoid complaints.

60: Evaluation

We all know that evaluation can be a source for happiness or disappointment. This will depend mainly on the employee's performance. I want here to focus on the **evaluation process**: is it clear, transparent and fair? This will increase the happiness level or at least minimize the disappointment.

It is necessary for managers to **discuss** the evaluation with employees and provide all related comments. Evaluation is not only providing negative comments, but also **appreciating** an employee's achievements and efforts. Evaluation shouldn't be done only at the end of the year, but **during the year** since the objective is to improve not to punish.

61: Job Performance

Every employee should ask himself about his job performance. Although it is the role of managers to monitor and evaluate employees' job performance, **the employee** should care about it also.

The main way to decide the **level of job performance** for any employee is through measuring the achievement of objectives and performance of assigned tasks. Managers should always **encourage** employees for a better job performance and continuously inform if any challenges are there.

Employees with a **high level of job performance** are always happier compared to those with low performance. This is because high performance means more appreciation, trust and higher chances for promotion.

62: Trainings

Big organizations care about trainings as they are an important factor to **develop** their employees. Trainings are essential for improving skills, gaining knowledge, closing gaps and learning from others.

Trainings can be **inside or outside** the organization. Employees will be happy if they get required training related to their jobs or any other kind of training which will be useful to improve their performance in their job roles.

Some organizations will **plan** trainings for the next year and give a chance for employees to choose whatever training is useful for them with approval of direct managers. **Effectiveness** and well-organized training is considered important.

63: Learning Programs

Learning programs are giving opportunities to employees for getting **specific certificates** or to continue their university studies. Having these opportunities will increase the level of employees' happiness.

These programs will finally improve the organization since the selected employees will gain **new knowledge.** They will then seek to use this knowledge to improve something in the organization.

Sending employees **to other countries** is also considered as learning programs. This is usually done for leaders to see best practices of other countries or organizations. Also, sometimes some employees are sent to learn new technologies which is expected to be applied in the organization.

64: Fairness

Fairness is one of the most important things that employees look in any organization. It is a main source for employees' happiness or disappointment. Fairness is important to be **applied** in everything such as appreciation, nominations, awards, promotions, evaluations, punishments and warnings...etc.

All **policies and regulations** should ensure fairness while applying them. Also, fairness is important while considering **males and females** meaning that each gender should be treated fairly.

Ensuring fairness is mainly the **responsibility** of leaders and mangers in addition to those who prepare and apply policies. Special cases are there always but they should be limited.

65: Ladies

Fairness is important at work. There should be some **special services** provided for ladies. We are not talking here about salaries, awards or promotions but things which are concerned with female staff.

In general, an organization should ensure that female employees feel **safe and secured** at work. Ladies need **policies** related to maternity leaves and nursing periods where they need to be at a healthy environment and close to their babies after delivery.

They also need some **activities** and programs which are more female related. Some organizations create **committees** for ladies to take care of organizing those activities and programs.

66: People of Determinations

There is a worldwide care about people of determinations*
nowadays. Many **policies and rules** are established to serve
them. The number of these people is slowly increasing in
organizations, and so it is important to have all required
facilities for them. This is besides applying **fairness**.

Organizations should conduct **awareness** for other staff
to know how to deal with this category. In general, people of
determinations should feel that they are **part** of the
organization and there is no difference between them and
others.

Some organizations establish **special committees** to serve
this category which shall increase their happiness.

* It was decided to call this category in the UAE as people
of determinations instead of disabilities.

67: Family

It is impossible to **separate** family issues from work. If an employee has an issue with his family it will surely affect work. Organizations should take care about families of an employee as much as possible. Some organizations do that through **providing some services** for an employee's family such as health insurance, air tickets, school fees, nurseries...etc. The organization can also invite employee families to attend some activities and programs.

Leaders and managers should also **support** and be **flexible** with any employee having family issues. Employees will feel happy when they know that the organization is **caring** about their family also.

68: Transparency

Transparency is another important value which employees want to see in their organizations. Transparency doesn't mean that everything should be known by all employees since there will be some confidential matters. We are talking here about aspects which will **directly affect** the employees such as policies, processes, evaluation…etc.

If policies and processes are **clear and well applied**, the level of complaints will be less. However, imagine that suddenly a new technology was selected to be implemented or the process of promotion in HR is not clear. Immediately, the employees will start to complain and ask: Why there is no transparency?

69: Respect

Respect is what every employee wants to feel in the organization. Without this respect many things won't go right. Respect is **multi-directional** among employees of different levels and their managers. Employees will be happy when they feel that they are respected from their leaders and managers.

Respect mainly comes while **dealing with others**, but also there should be respect while reading, listening or requesting any opinions or suggestions. **Smiling and using nice words** is also a kind form of respect to others.

Respecting others is not something occasional but it should be part of an organization's **culture**.

70: New Technologies

We can notice clearly the **feelings** of any employee if we ask them regarding usage of technology in the organization. Using old technology might make the employee satisfied especially if such technology is serving its purpose. However, it is for sure that this organization will be **far behind others** by not adopting new technologies.

As we are now in a small world, any new technology **announced will spread quickly**. If this technology is found to be effective, developed organizations will run fast to apply it. Employees will feel happy to see that their organizations are **applying new technologies** especially if they were effective and useful.

71: New Trends

We are witnessing a huge revolution in science and information and the result produces new trends announced in short periods of time.

Currently, we are hearing about Artificial Intelligence, smart applications, Big Data, Block Chain…etc. Applying these trends in the organization will provide employees a feeling that they are **part of this revolution** and the organization is not far away from big leading ones in the world.

Compare this with an employee who **doesn't know** what are these new trends or none of them are applied in the organization. Will the employee be happy especially that news and implementation of these trends are everywhere?

72: Open Door Policy

Open door is a known policy where leaders and managers will have **open time** for any employee to discuss any matter related to work. The policy will be successful if leaders and managers build **trust** with employees; otherwise, no one will knock the leader's or manager's doors.

Famous organizations **encourage** leaders and managers to apply this policy. Successful leaders and managers don't need to apply this policy since their doors **are always open** as they encourage employees to raise any issue or discuss any matter with them. This is besides **seeing them always** with employees during any event or occasion.

73: Open Discussion

Open discussion is conducted usually by top leaders or department heads with employees. In these open discussions which could be individual or group, many personal or work-related issues shall be raised. On the other hand, leaders or mangers will deliver some **important messages** to employees.

It is important to have these open discussions **regularly** since employees usually won't have much chance to meet top leaders and managers due to their busy schedule. Also, leaders, managers and employees should not build **any negative impact** about these discussions; otherwise, the next time nobody will attend or important issues shall be hidden by employees.

74: Safety

An employees' safety should be one of the organization's **main concerns**. All necessary tools, processes and mechanisms should be available to support safety in the organization.

Safety culture is important to be spread among employees. This can be done through awareness and messages delivered through different channels. Also, following **international safety standards** will support applying better safety environment in the organization.

Availability of **first aiders** and **first aid tools** in the right places is a must and more important. There should be a **clear process** of dealing with accidents or injuries. Having all of this will surely raise happiness of employees.

75: Security

Security has become one of the **hottest topics** in the world due to different threats and attacks. Employees should feel that their organization is **really secured**. Imagine the feeling of the employees if they discovered that their PCs are hacked, they can't access information or emails or there are possibilities of threats targeting the organization. All of this will be a source of **worry or disappointment** for the employees.

Building **security culture** is important and should be a priority for the organization. Employees themselves have a major role in securing their information in addition to a dedicated security team or department.

76: Job Security

Besides securing organization's information and assets, one of employees' most important concerns is to secure their jobs. Imagine an employee coming to office every day expecting that this day will be the last day in this organization. What will be his **feelings** and what will be the **productivity** level?

Leaders should always send **clear messages** to all employees that their jobs are secure and there is no need to worry about future as long as the organization is going in the right direction.

It is important also to stop and warn **negative employees** whose main role is to scare others especially in a bad or a crisis situation.

77: Balance

One of the golden rules to achieve happiness in life is balance. Balance in work means to **give each thing its weight**. In fact, there are many objectives required from employees where most of them are related to work. However, there can be some objectives not related to their direct work, but it is still equally important such as being a member of a committee outside the department.

Balance requires **planning and prioritizing things**. Also, balance between **work and personal life** is important to achieve happiness.

Employees who come late to home every day without having a chance to sit with their family must rethink and redesign their life.

78: Car Parking

How many employees will be **worried** if they know that they won't find a parking or they will search for it for a long time? Car parking might not be considered a priority for the organization, but it will surely affect the level of employees' happiness. As such, it should be one of the considerations which should be taken care by leaders.

I have seen a lot of **complaints and suggestions** from employees regarding car parking which means that they really want this facility to be available. Some organization locations might be near to a public transportation station which is also good and can save a lot of hassle.

79: Facilities

Employees like to have facilities in the organization. Facilities can be gyms, restaurants or bakeries, playing centers, nurseries, ATM machines...etc. **The more facilities available**, the happier the employees will be. In fact, these facilities are made to make employees happy.

Leaders should always care about **employees' requirements**. This can be known through surveys, open discussions, direct feedback from employees or seeing other organizations' best practices.

One important notice is that these facilities should **not take much time** from employees. Otherwise, it can have a bad impact on the main work and can lead to certain decisions that would defeat the initial purpose of providing those facilities.

80: Cleanness

What if someone went to office and found it full of dust or waste? What if wash rooms were unclean? What if the meeting room smell was unacceptable? I think the point is clear. Cleanness is important for all employees and it will surely affect their level of happiness.

Employees want to see their offices, wash rooms, meeting rooms, elevators…etc. clean with nice smells; otherwise, there will be **complains** or at least bad feelings and discomfort during work.

It will be valuable to bring a **cleaning company** to look after organization's cleanness. This should be besides **employees' role** to maintain cleanness.

81: Health Insurance

Health insurance is one of the benefits which some organizations provide to their employees. Sometimes, it depends on employee's grade to get the **level of benefits** from this insurance and whether it will cover the employee's family or not. Still, it is something worth to many employees.

Organization should also seek to provide more **benefits** related to health insurance such as the maximum amount allowed for each employee and the range of hospitals and pharmacies. All of this will increase employee's happiness level. Also, it is important to note that employees **should not misuse** this insurance.

82: Compensations and Benefits

Many organizations provide a variety of compensations and benefits to their employees which make them happy and attract new employees.

Organizations who seek to increase employees' happiness tend to **innovate** in these compensations and benefits. Some do **agreements** with hotels or restaurants for special offers for their employees. Others provide special leaves or early leaving from office in some occasions. Also, some extend the benefits to **employees' families** which is valuable to many employees.

The moment an employee feels that the organization is **caring** about him, his level of happiness will be increased and his productivity will be higher.

83: Loyalty

There is a **link** between loyalty and happiness. Although not all loyal employees are happy since there are different reasons for loyalty. However, happy employees are **more likely** to be loyal to organization.

Organizations **make sure** that their employees are loyal since they don't want their employees, especially the excellent ones to leave. In order to ensure that, one of the main things is to conduct and maintain happiness programs for the employees.

Happy employees will usually stay in the organization for a longer time and in some cases until the end of service or retirement. **Loyal employees** will be more productive and happier.

84: Free Time at Work

This matter is **not agreed** among leaders. Some think that work time should be completely for work and some others prefer to provide free time for employees since it will **recharge** them or will increase their happiness level.

I'm with the second team if the working hours are somehow long; however, free time can also be available in shorter working hours but in a **controlled manner**.

The main idea is to define the **objective** of this free time and to be clear for all leaders, managers and employees. **Trust** between leaders and employees is an important factor if this free time is assigned.

85: First Day at Work

How many of us **remember** the first day of his work and what was the impression taken from the organization from that first day? Some organizations **care** about employee's first day through nice gifts and arranging their offices with all needed facilities. This will give a great **impression** for the employees and surely, they will be happy.

The opposite situation exists unfortunately in some organizations. The employee doesn't know where to go with no office or any facilities. What will be his feelings?

First day at work is important and should be taken care by organization's HR and related departments.

86: IT

IT (Information Technology) related things are important for any organization. It has an important role and any problem in it will affect employee's happiness.

There are many **roles** for IT such as providing PCs or laptops and smart devices for employees. More importantly is the **support and availability** at all times.

Having a **strong and secured network** is another important factor. Employees don't want their network to be disturbed or hacked any time. It is important to have an IT support through different channels such as phones, emails, systems…etc. Also, providing latest systems with their updates is essential.

87: Absence from Work

Circumstances can happen to any employee to make him absent from work. It is where the **role of the managers** is to ask for reasons for this absence and not take any negative action before confirming the situation.

Even in case of unreasonable excuse for absence, there should be always **positive actions** from managers by advising and stating the importance of any employee and the effect of being absent from work for no reason.

This is again something related to **culture** which managers should learn and be trained by the organization. Employees should feel happy even when they are away from work.

88: Warning Letters

Warning letters is a **punishment tool** used by many organizations due to breaking rules or low performance. This warning should be used as a **last option** after spending all other possible solutions with the employee.

Warning letters will surely affect happiness of an employee. The role of managers is very important while issuing warning letters. The **objective and justifications** should be very clear so that the employee will know that he/she deserves this warning letter.

The manager should also explain to the employee that this warning letter **is not the end of life** but can be a starting point for improved performance.

89: Leaves

Leaves are the **right** of any employee in the organization. Number of leave days will differ among organizations. One important note here is not to **reject** any leave without reasonable justification especially if the employee is away from his original country.

Sometimes, many employees want to take leave at the same time. Here comes the role of the managers to **organize**. Also, it is important to have an advance plan for annual leaves from the beginning of the year.

There can be many kinds of leaves within the organization. It is important to have a **clear policy** for leaves to avoid any conflict.

90: Benchmarking

Benchmarking is simply **comparing** ourselves as an organization to others either by visiting them or being visited by others. It has many benefits to individuals and organization.

If the organization is being continuously benchmarked, it will give a feeling that it is among the **leading organizations** and a **good model** for others which will make employees happy and proud.

On the other hand, if the organization is benchmarking with others, it will show that it wants to **improve** and **gather knowledge** which will make employees happy also. Staying neutral and not caring about the current position is a negative indication which employees don't like.

91: Flexible Hours

Some organizations provide their employees with a flexible hour option. It is a nice option since it will **reduce pressure** on the employee to come early in the morning at the exact time especially for locations having traffic jams.

Also, some employees prefer to stay more during the afternoon or evening rather than coming early in the morning and leaving early afternoon. The **objective** of the flexible hour is to make employees happy and comfortable at their work.

Leaders should ensure that work is **not affected** with a flexible hour option especially if work is related to external customers. **Policies** can be established for organization's purpose.

92: Working from Home

Another option provided for some employees is working from home. It is applied for some jobs where employee's presence at work is **not essential**. Again, it should be known for all that the objective of this option is to increase employee happiness. **Policies** are needed but should not affect happiness.

I think that working from home is good provided that **all objectives are met**; still the presence of those employees are needed **periodically** in order to be close from the work environment and be aware about any new events or rules. In addition, it is important is to have direct communication with leaders and managers.

93: Help Desk

Organizations have several help desks in different ways for **several purposes**. There can be help desk for HR related issues, for technical issues and so on.

Employees usually **use** these help desks a lot. In case it is a number, there should be clear, simple and a different language menu to follow. After choosing the required one, there should be fast response all the time. Even if the employee's problem or clarifications are not answered, there should be **support** for the employee for the next steps.

The same thing should exist for any other help desk type: easy, clear, fast and simple.

94: Job Autonomy

Job autonomy means **being independent** or having freedom during work. It is important for any employee to feel that he is not monitored or restricted all the time. Some managers are "micromanagers" who tend to control all details of the work and used to give permission before any movement even if going to wash rooms!!! This will surely affect employees' happiness and performance.

Providing **suggestions and opinions** should be open always but in good ways. There should be always **trust** between managers and employees. One of the factors for building this trust is feeling some freedom and independence during work.

95: Purpose

If we ask any employee in the organization, **why are you here?** Whoever knows the answer will feel proud and happy. The other group's feelings are known also.

Knowing the purpose is important for employees. This is mainly the role of **managers** to ensure the effectiveness of the role of any employee. The moment that any employee **feels** that he is not important, his productivity and happiness will be affected.

It is also important to know the **organization's purpose**. Why does it exist? And what is its importance? This will make the employees feel that they are important and they will be proud of their work.

96: Solving Problems

Problems keep arising every day and it is something **common** in every organization. Employees care about the **ways** these problems are solved. Whether they are really solved or not, they are just being covered or are solved partially. Also, who is involved in solving problems? Is it just the leaders and managers or other employees are also involved?

It is important to **train** employees about **scientific ways** for solving problems. More importantly, it is **involving** them or taking their advice or knowledge in their area of expertise.

Nobody likes problems, but employees should be taught to take these problems as **opportunities** and chances to improve and learn more.

97: Decision Making

Another important skill for the leaders of any organization is decision making which affects directly or indirectly on employee's happiness.

Many questions are raised before or after any decision. Who made this decision? Is it a group's or an individual's decision? How long it took to make such decisions?

Having clear answers to these questions will make the employees more satisfied and happier.

Learning **different ways** for taking best and right decisions is important, but more importantly is the way of **applying** them. Also, the time for taking decisions is important whether it is urgent or can be delayed.

98: Escaping from Deciding

Some leaders and managers escape from taking decisions that will have negative impacts on employee's happiness.

I notice this negative effect when some employees need a critical decision related to work such as continuing or stopping something and they need their managers or leader decision then they wait for long time without any feedback that will cause employees to become stress and worry.

Instead, leaders and mangers should provide decisions either immediately for urgent and important cases or after some time if it needs more discussions, yet the time of decision should be clear for employees.

99: Resignations

Resignations can happen in any organization due to **several reasons**, but surely it will be less in organizations which have a **high** happiness level among their employees.

It is the role of the organization to study the **causes** of employees' resignations. Some studies are stating that **managers** are the **biggest reason** for employees to leave the organization, so it is important to focus on leaders and managers to care about their employees.

Reducing the level of resignation is important since it will maintain an organization's main assets: the employees, especially the expert and distinguished ones. Also, it will give a sign that the organization is caring about its employees.

100: Internal or External

I wanted to conclude the happiness tools with a question: **which is more important?** Internal happiness which is something within the employee or external happiness which is what organizations should create? This is a debatable topic but **both of them are important to be considered**.

Internal happiness will keep the employees motivated regardless of what the organization is doing, however, there is an important role for the organization to increase happiness of its employees through different tools.

I think that internal happiness is more important but it needs more efforts. At the same time, organizations should train their employees to always sustain happiness.

Conclusion

Happiness is one of the **most important subjects** nowadays and almost all organizations are focusing on it.

Although I mentioned **100 ways** in this book, there are a **lot of other tools** which can support and increase employees' happiness since there are continuous studies, researches and different initiatives regarding happiness being carried out.

I want to remind everyone about my objective of this book. It is mainly to open the reader's mind about the mentioned ways without going into a lot of depth giving the opportunity to readers to search more about each way. I hope **I added value** for all who read this book.